westlife

OMNIBUS PRESS

Cover & book designed by Phil Gambrill.
Picture research by Nikki Lloyd.

ISBN: 0.7119.8280.5
Order No: OP48186

Exclusive Distributors
Book Sales Limited,
8/9 Frith Street,
London W1V 5TZ, UK.

Music Sales Corporation,
257 Park Avenue South,
New York, NY 10010, USA.

The Five Mile Press,
22 Summit Road,
Noble Park,
Victoria 3174, Australia.

To the Music Trade only:
Music Sales Limited,
8/9 Frith Street,
London W1V 5TZ, UK.

Photo credits:
Craig Barritt / Retna:5, 7;
Patrick Ford / Redferns: 1;
Fotex / Olly / Redferns: poster;
John Gladwin / All Action: 24;
Mick Hutson / Redferns: 11t;
Arjan Kleton / Sunshine / Retna: 22;
Michael Linssen / Redferns: 20;
London Features International;
back cover, 4, 9, 11b, 12, 14, 15, 16,
17, 18, 19, 21, 23, 25, 29, 30, 31;
Sue Moore / All Action: 8;
Doug Peters / All Action: 32;
Brian Rasic: front cover, 2/3, 26, 27, 28;
Clemens Rikken Sunshine / Retna: 13;
Jim Sharp / Redferns: 10;
Ian Yates / Retna: 6.

Every effort has been made to trace
the copyright holders of the photographs
in this book but one or two were unreachable.
We would be grateful if the photographers
concerned would contact us.

Printed in Great Britain.

A catalogue record for this book is available
from the British Library.

www.omnibuspress.com

the westlife
story

The Westlife story started in 1998 in the North West of Ireland – a small town called Sligo, which had a vibrant youth theatre scene. That year's production was *Grease*, and after the last show the cast were partying in traditional style. Three local teenagers – Shane Filan, Kian Egan and Mark Feehily, members of the T Birds gang in the musical – were so happy they burst into song, and went down so well they decided to form a band. Recruiting three other hopefuls named Derrick, Graham and Michael, they called themselves Six As One and played their first gig, a half-hour selection of boy-band cover versions, at the local Southern Hotel.

Six As One soon became very popular in Sligo and showed they had ambitions beyond just copying other acts when they wrote a song called 'Together Girl Forever'. They recorded this for a small independent record label, who released it under the new name of IOU... not, as it turned out, the last name they'd go under before they hit the top. A year older than the others, ever-confident Shane quickly showed himself to be the leading light, and remains the spokesperson of the band today.

A copy of the CD reached Boyzone's manager, Louis Walsh, courtesy of Shane's mum Mae. Impressed by what he heard, he quickly auditioned the sixsome and, as a result, gave them their first showcase gig – opening for the Backstreet Boys in Dublin. Their 15-minute routine went well, but it was just as well the old name had gone because Louis Walsh, now their manager, wanted them to slim down to a Boyzone-style five-piece. Derrick, who looked rather more mature than the others, was the unlucky one to miss out.

Boyzone were understandably interested to hear of their manager's new protégés... and it was natural that lead singer Ronan Keating should drop by to lend some words of advice from someone who'd been there, done that and whose face had sold thousands of T-shirts! He got on well with them – so well, in fact, that he was quickly installed as co-manager. Talent scout was a role he'd play again on TV's *Get Your Act Together*; but this was no talent show, this was for real. And reality struck again when Graham, nearly 22 to the others' teens, was told his face didn't fit the image.

By the time auditions for a replacement were held at the Red Box in Dublin, the buzz had got round about 'the next Boyzone'. No fewer than 300 young men queued round the block for the chance to impress, and were narrowed down first to six and then to two – Bryan McFadden and Nicky Byrne. It was impossible to split the pair, whose singing and dancing talents were equally impressive. In the end, both were selected and another band member, Michael, departed.

Shane, the band's unofficial leader, admits telling his three friends they'd been dropped from the ranks was the hardest thing he'd ever had to face. "It was so ruthless," he grimaces, "but that's the business. Two of the guys aren't friendly with us any more and I can't blame them. I mean, we kicked them out…"

The two newcomers couldn't have been more different in background. Nicky had been a budding footballer, spending time with Leeds United and gaining Eire international honours at 15 and 16, but failed to quite grow to the requisite height for a goalkeeper so was left to look for another route to stardom. Bryan, by contrast, had been in stage school – the same one Boyzone's Mikey Graham went to – since the age of four and was fulfilling a lifelong dream. The pair knew each other, having met on the karaoke circuit: "I used to sing Boyzone songs," Nicky later recalled, "and Bryan used to sing Backstreet Boys songs."

It was now July, and the new five-piece line-up won further fame when they headlined 2FM Radio's Beat On The Streets roadshow which toured Ireland for eight sunny summer weekends. It would prove the ideal springboard to national fame, and gave them the opportunity to fine-tune their act as they sought that all-important record deal. When it came, it was with BMG/RCA, the label that had given a first taste of fame to artists as legendary as Elvis Presley and David Bowie. It had also, more recently, been home to Take That. The demise of Manchester's mega boy-band had left a big gap… but these five Irish boys had no doubt they could fill it!

It had been agreed they'd not sign to Polydor, Boyzone's label, to avoid any conflict of interest – but that didn't mean the lads couldn't open for Ronan and Co on their upcoming UK tour. They would play this under the new name of Westside, a logo Louis had spotted on the side of a skip. There was just time for four numbers each night – 'Swear It Again', 'Flying Without Wings', 'Everybody Knows' and 'If I Let You Go' – but these made such an impression on the fans that Westside soon found themselves on the cover of teen magazines just four short months after they'd formed. It had been a whirlwind rise to fame, and it was far from over.

The place on the *Smash Hits* Roadshow in November, following in the footsteps of Five and playing alongside the likes of S Club 7, A1 and Billie, took them to Birmingham, Glasgow, Newcastle, Manchester and Sheffield, and helped them win that magazine's Best New Act award the following month. It really had been a remarkable rise to fame. "On the day of the previous year's *Smash Hits* party," Shane revealed, "we released our independent single with our last group and played to 60 people. Now look at us – it's incredible."

Not that it had been easy coping with the 24-hour pressures of pop stardom. They'd had bust-ups and arguments along the way, as all teenagers do, but emerged the stronger for it – and such was their team spirit that they asked for six copies of the *Smash Hits* trophy, one for each member of the band plus their manager, Louis Walsh. Ronan already had a mantelpiece full of 'em!

Next stop was recording their debut single – and the vote went to 'Swear It Again', the song that had received the best reaction on tour. But nothing else was quite as simple: another group in America had been discovered with the same name, so on the eve of their first release they were re-christened Westlife. This, of course, made no difference whatsoever to the single's success, and just seven days after it appeared in the shops 'Swear It Again' was sitting pretty at the top of the charts!

The band was much in demand for promotional appearances, but never forgot to include good causes in their agenda. As they celebrated their first Number 1 in early May 1999, they paid an unannounced visit to Streatham Hill and Clapham High School in London to put their weight behind an anti-violence campaign. "We young people should do all we can to help each other," said Bryan.

Next came 'If I Let You Go', released in the middle of August and the ideal theme for a summer holiday romance. It repeated its predecessor's success, but who should it knock off the top but co-manager Ronan Keating and his film-theme solo debut! The track was refreshingly different, an acoustic guitar-powered mid-pacer that showed another side to the 'Life. It was very Backstreet Boys-ish, but the tempo would slow again for their next chartbound shot.

By the time 'Flying Without Wings' made its bow in late October, it was almost accepted Westlife would make it a hat-trick of best-sellers. Amazingly, the song had been written with teenage country diva LeAnn Rimes in mind before the lads' record company persuaded its writers, Steve Mac and Wayne Hector (who'd also penned 'Swear It Again'), to wing it Westlife's way. Never mind LeAnn Rimes… Christina Aguilera had to put her genie back in its bottle as the Irish lads Riverdanced their merry way to the top, leaving even the Backstreet Boys' new release trailing in their wake. It was a long way from that four-song guest spot in Dublin… the tables had been well and truly turned!

Next came Westlife's long-awaited debut album – and even though it opened with the self-same three hits people had been buying in their thousands, it was still tipped for the top. Everyone held their breath… but 'Steptacular', which had hit Number 1 the previous week, made it unlucky 13th November for the lads. Even so, they were delighted that Five couldn't leapfrog them… and by its third week in the charts *Westlife* had turned platinum with over 300,000 copies sold in the UK alone.

The songs came from many different sources. Five were written by 'Flying Without Wings' creators Mac and Hector, while the team of Topham, Twigg and Ellington (who contributed 'Change The World') were best-known for penning many of Steps' smashes. There were two unusual cover versions too – 'More Than Words', a big ballad hit in 1991 for US heavy-metallers Extreme, and 'Seasons In The Sun', of which much more would soon be heard.

With The Spice Girls taking a break from Christmas singles, the chance was there for Westlife to make it four chart-toppers in a row when December came around – and they did so in style! 'I Have A Dream'/'Seasons In The Sun' was a pretty good bet from the word go, not least because both songs had been hits before. Suitably, 'I Have A Dream' had been Abba's Christmas record exactly two decades before (though it only reached Number 2), while 'Seasons In The Sun' was a 1974 chart-topper – well before any of Westlife had even been thought of! – for Canadian singer Terry Jacks. The lyrics, about a man looking death in the face, were specially poignant for Nicky, who'd lost his cousin earlier in the year… yet, as ever, he and Westlife delivered in their usual professional style.

By now, the boys were rubbing shoulders with the stars, and were delighted when Status Quo, those veteran long-haired rockers, came up to ask for their autographs for their kids! "I was about to ask for *their* autographs for my dad!" laughed a delighted Mark. Rumours were rife that Boyzone were to go their separate ways, leaving Westlife to inherit their mantle as Ireland's undisputed Number 1 boy band. But when Ronan and the lads vowed to carry on, no-one was more delighted than the 'Life, Shane admitting they'd not have come so far so soon without their example. "Ronan said that it took them at least two years to get where they are now… he's learned from the mistakes they made and helped us avoid them. People take more notice of Irish bands now, thanks to Boyzone."

And there was little doubt the boys would stay where their roots were. "No matter how famous we get," Nicky confirmed, "I know I'll always live in Ireland. At the end of the day it's my home. But you never know – if we make enough money I may get a place in London as well!" Talking of Britain's capital city, Nicky had once been told by a fortune teller he'd play at Wembley. He naturally assumed it would be as a footballer… but when Westlife played the Arena in 1999, selling it out in the process, there was no prouder lad.

The first single of the new millennium was another slowie, 'Fool Again', which arrived in February 2000. With those creamy harmonies decorating a memorable chorus, this was classic Westlife – and made it five hits from the album. Not that anyone could complain: with 17 tracks and 65 minutes of music, *Westlife* more than deserved its multi-platinum status. As 1999 ended, it was poised to break the million mark in UK sales alone – and that made them megastars in anybody's language!

As for the future, all five Westlifers have agreed not to get married or have kids for five years. "We've got plenty of time to do that stuff," says Shane, "we're only young." So it's bad news for anyone with romantic designs on the famous five… but if it means five years of great music, we won't be complaining. In fact, it sounds like a 'Life sentence!

westlife
factfile

kian

Full Name
Kian John Francis Egan

Date of birth
29th April 1980

Place of birth
Sligo, Ireland

Zodiac Sign
Taurus

Height
5ft 10ins

Colour of eyes
Blue

Colour of hair
Blond

Family
Three brothers and three sisters

Any tattoos
A Chinese symbol meaning spirit/soul

Hobbies
Snooker, pitch and putt

Likes
Performing on stage, having a good
night out and being in Westlife

Dislikes
Sushi and rude people

Favourite sport
Basketball

Favourite male singer
Brian Littrell

Favourite female singer
Celine Dion

Favourite food
Steak and Chips

Favourite soft drink
7 Up

Favourite place to visit
USA

Favourite men's perfume
Joop

Favourite women's perfume
Too many to mention

Favourite football team
Liverpool

Favourite song
'Baby One More Time'
by Britney Spears

Motto
'Treat everybody as you want
to be treated'

bryan

Name
Bryan Nicholas McFadden

Date of birth
12th April 1980

Zodiac Sign
Aries

Place of birth
Dublin

Colour of eyes
Blue

Colour of hair
Browny blond

Height
6ft 1in

Any tattoos
Not yet

Family
Sister called Susan and
a dog called Chip

Hobbies
Singing, dancing, music, football

Likes
Music, females and
spending money

Dislikes
School, reading, writing

Favourite sport
Soccer

Favourite male singer
Brian Littrell

Favourite female singer
Mariah Carey

Favourite food
A fry up from the
Carlton Cafe in Sligo

Favourite soft drink
Cola Light

Favourite place to visit
USA

Favourite men's perfume
D&G

Favourite women's perfume
Cool Water

Favourite football team
Manchester United

Favourite song
'Something Stupid' by Frank Sinatra

Motto
'Live life today and deal with
tomorrow when it comes!'

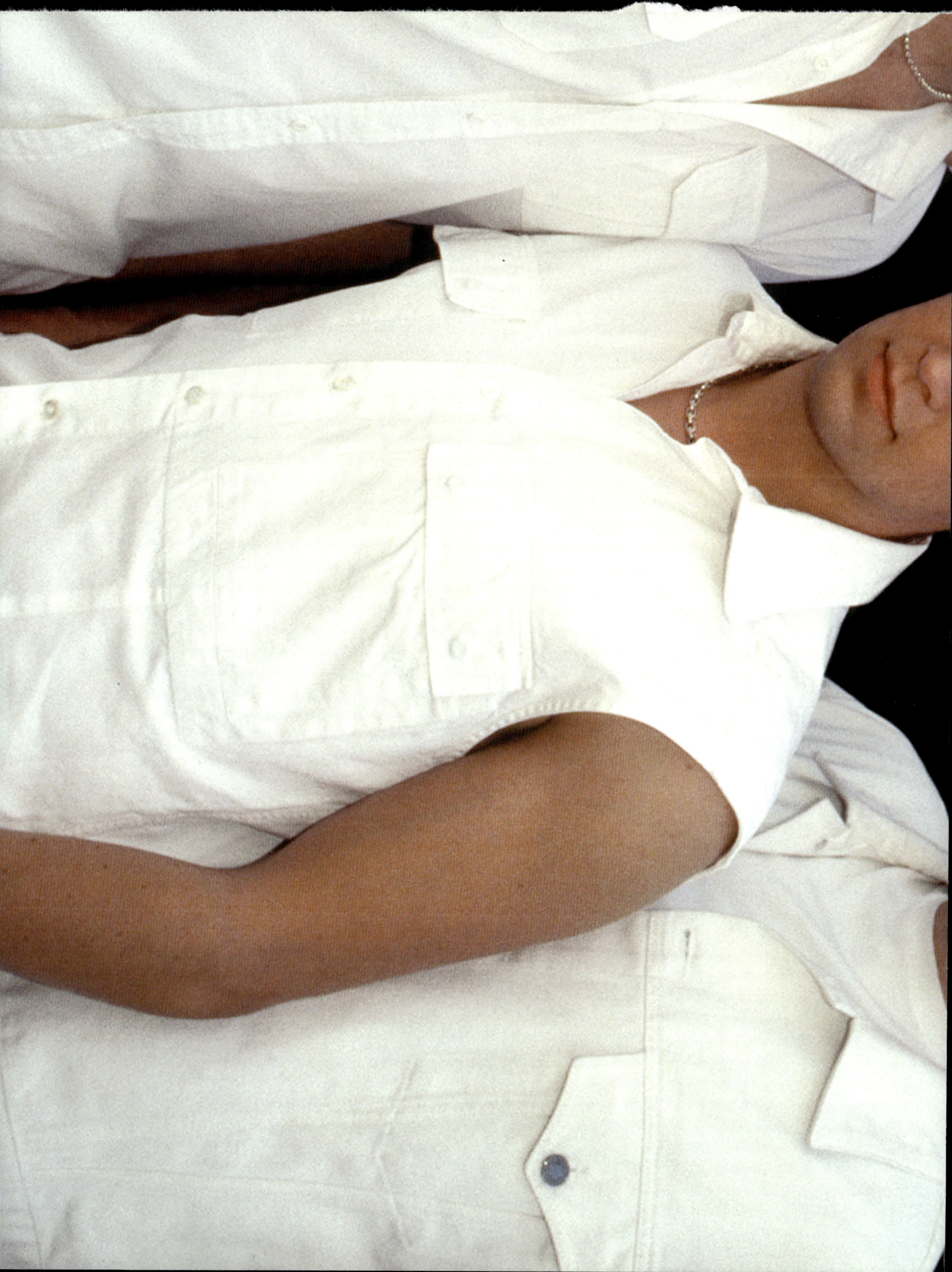

mark

Full Name
Mark Michael Patrick Feehily

Date of birth
28th May 1980

Zodiac Sign
Gemini

Place of birth
Sligo, Ireland

Height
5ft 11ins

Colour of eyes
Blue

Colour of hair
Dark brown

Family
Two brothers

Hobbies
Snooker, chilling out

Likes
Chillin' with his mates,
singing and partying

Dislikes
Being tied down,
having too much on his plate,
narrow-minded people, smoking

Favourite sports
Football, tennis

Favourite male singer
Michael Jackson

Favourite female singer
Mariah Carey

Favourite food
Steak and chips

Favourite soft drink
Lemon Fanta

Favourite place to visit
Home

Favourite men's perfume
Hugo Boss

Favourite women's perfume
Calvin Klein

Favourite football team
Liverpool

Favourite song
'Man In The Mirror'
by Michael Jackson and
'Without You' by Mariah Carey

Motto
'Money isn't everything –
happiness is'

shane

Full Name	Shane Steven Filan
Date of birth	5th July 1979
Zodiac sign	Cancer
Place of birth	Sligo, Ireland
Height	5ft 9ins
Colour of eyes	Hazel green
Colour of hair	Dark brown
Family	Three brothers and three sisters
Any tattoos	No
Hobbies	Horse riding, snooker, pitch and putt
Likes	Shopping, girls, going out with his friends, horses and singing
Dislikes	Insects, snakes, rude people
Favourite sports	Soccer, horse riding
Favourite male singer	George Michael
Favourite female singer	Mariah Carey
Favourite food	Spaghetti
Favourite soft drink	Coca-Cola
Favourite place to visit	Tenerife
Favourite men's perfume	Polo
Favourite women's perfume	Chloe
Favourite football team	Liverpool
Favourite song	'I Believe I Can Fly' by R Kelly
Motto	'You only live once, so live a good life!'

nicky

Full Name
Nicholas Bernard James Adam Byrne

Date of birth
9th October 1978

Zodia Sign
Libra

Place of birth
Dublin

Height
5ft 9½ ins

Colour of eyes
Blue

Colour of hair
Medium brown

Family
One sister and one brother

Any tattoos
None – yet

Hobbies
Football and snooker

Likes
Football, eating out, shopping and
travelling home to see his family

Dislikes
Smoking and nasty people

Favourite sports
Soccer, snooker

Favourite male singer
Phil Collins

Favourite female singer
Natalie Imbruglia

Favourite food
Sunday dinner

Favourite soft drink
Pepsi

Favourite place to visit
Caribbean, New York or Sydney

Favourite men's perfume
Dolce & Gabbana

Favourite women's perfume
CK Eternity

Favourite football team
Manchester United

Favourite song
'Flying Without Wings'
(by Westlife!)

Motto
'Never think anyone's better
than you, and never think you
are better than anyone else'

westlife

quotes

"Louis has Spice Girls-type names for us, but we're not telling you what they are 'cos we don't want everyone to start using them!"
mark

"I'll know I'm famous when my mum asks me for my autograph."
nicky

"Irish men are the most romantic in the world. We love treating girls to nice, romantic evenings, doing things like taking them to dinner, go and watch a video or go for a nice romantic stroll. The countryside in Ireland is very beautiful…"
shane

"I'll know I'm famous when I have five Ferraris, seven houses, Cameron Diaz on my arm and a little man following me with a huge bag of money!"
bryan

"The days are gone when you could just put five good-looking lads on stage and that'd be it. You need to be talented…"
kian

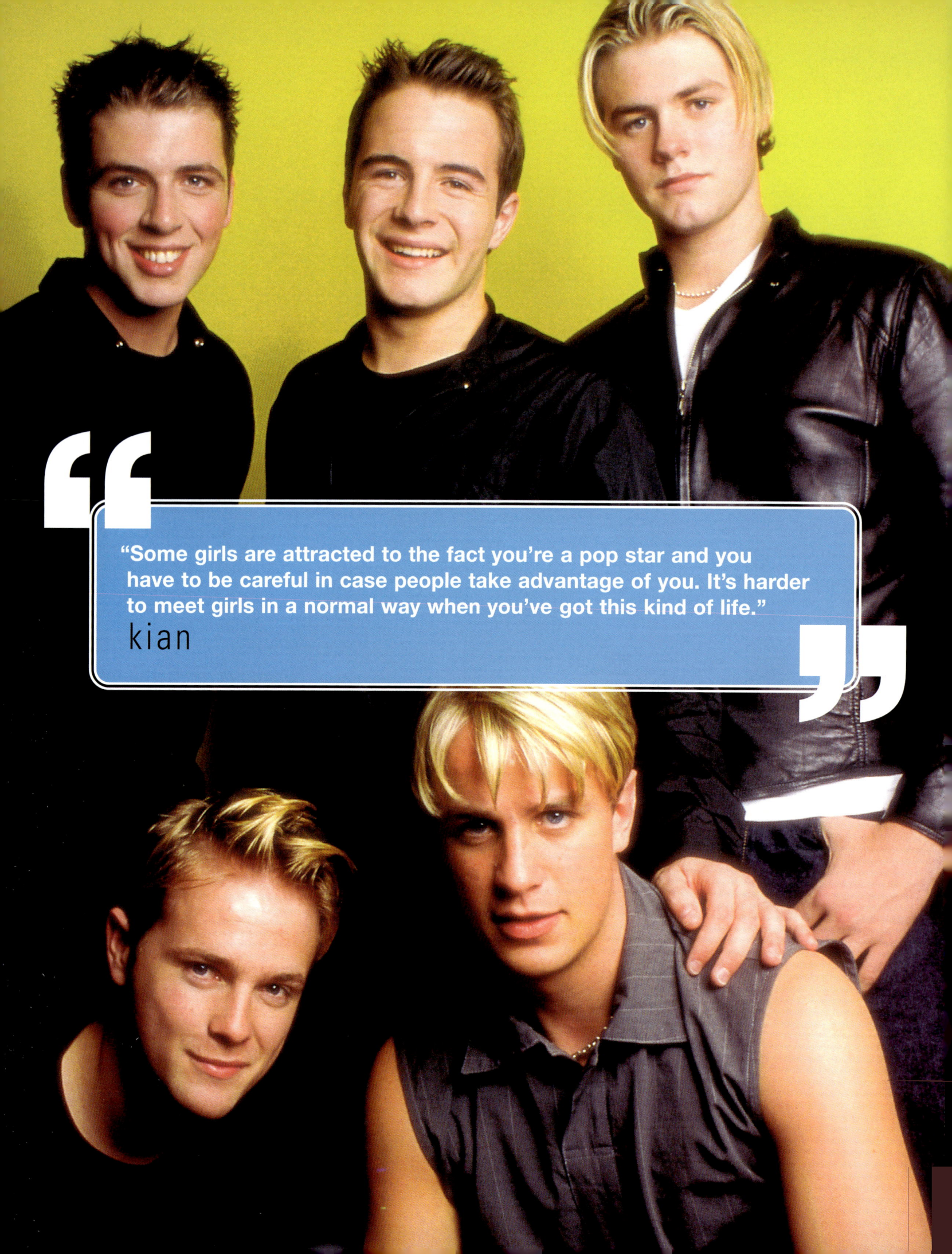

"Some girls are attracted to the fact you're a pop star and you have to be careful in case people take advantage of you. It's harder to meet girls in a normal way when you've got this kind of life."
kian

"It's hard to keep in touch with friends: I don't think people realise how little free time we get.
When you do get back to your hotel room, you're so knackered you just want to chill out.
Some people think we're too big to talk to them but it's nothing like that."
kian

"Me and Shane share on tour, so you can imagine what our hotel room's like – a bit like Beirut!"
bryan

"Fans aren't from a different planet – why should it be that, because they're into our music,
we can't be friends with them? It's the same when people ask us whether we'd date a fan –
of course we would."
mark

**"I went to an all boys' school and I was in the choir. One day we went to the girls' school
next door to sing with them and one of my mates had a rubber snake with him. I threw it at the
girls, who were all screaming and running round, and unfortunately got caught!"**
nicky

"I went away for a three-day rugby tournament and I forgot all my boxer shorts.
We were in the middle of nowhere and I had to wear the same pair day in, day in, day out,
even during the matches. They smelt after a while!"
shane

"I'd like to go car racing or clay pigeon shooting! I've got a good eye for it. I was really good at sports when I was younger."

bryan

"When I was at school I got lines for dropping a big squelchy, loud fart. My teacher, who was a priest, made me write 'I must not fart in class' 100 times. I left that school shortly afterwards."

bryan

"We were round Ronan's having dinner. One of his friends was having a drink and we swapped his short with a swig of vinegar. Then we started going 'Drink, drink, drink!' He did it, his face turned green and then he puked everywhere!"

bryan

"I was meeting my girlfriend's parents for the first time and trying to sound like the nicest little kid ever. They asked about my interests and I said, 'I like singing, dancing, acting and go-karting.' Their faces dropped and I got a huge lecture about the dangers of go-karting and warned never to take their daughter near a go-kart – it was *so* embarrassing."

mark

"This business is all about positive thinking, and you have to believe in yourself, think about all the good things you have. We all love what we do so much."

nicky

"Everyone argues from time to time, but we're all pulling together. We're still getting to know each other and know what we do and don't like and how far we can push each other."

shane

"When I broke up with my first serious girlfriend I was absolutely gutted. One night I was at this club, and of course, my ex-girlfriend was there. After a few drinks I got a little emotional and ended up just slumped in a corner crying my eyes out."

kian

"I like different kinds of girls. You know when you see someone that you could get on with...
if they're nice looking and have nice clothes on. But you have to see what they're like as a person."
mark

"It was at a party to celebrate our exam results; I must have been 15. It's one of those
nights when everyone goes out and goes mad. I was at this night-club called the Furnace
in Dublin, which is actually closed down now, and I must have had about 11 snogs.
I don't think it was any more than that!"
nicky

"I was caught speeding past a hospital doing 47 mph in a 30 mph zone. There were four of us in the
car and it was just after I passed my test. We were on our way to the Irish trials for rugby and were late,
so on the bigger roads I was probably going a lot faster. Luckily the cop loved rugby so he let me off,
although he wasn't too happy with my dodgy number plate."
shane

"Nicky's terrified about being stuck in a lift so I'm always dragging him into them,
jumping up and down, pretending it's stuck, anything just to freak him out! Actually...
I torment Nicky about most of his phobias!"
kian

"I collected *Discovery* magazine. Looking back it was such a boring thing to do cos it's all
about stuff like the Kings and Queens of England. I used to keep each copy stashed away in a file!"
bryan

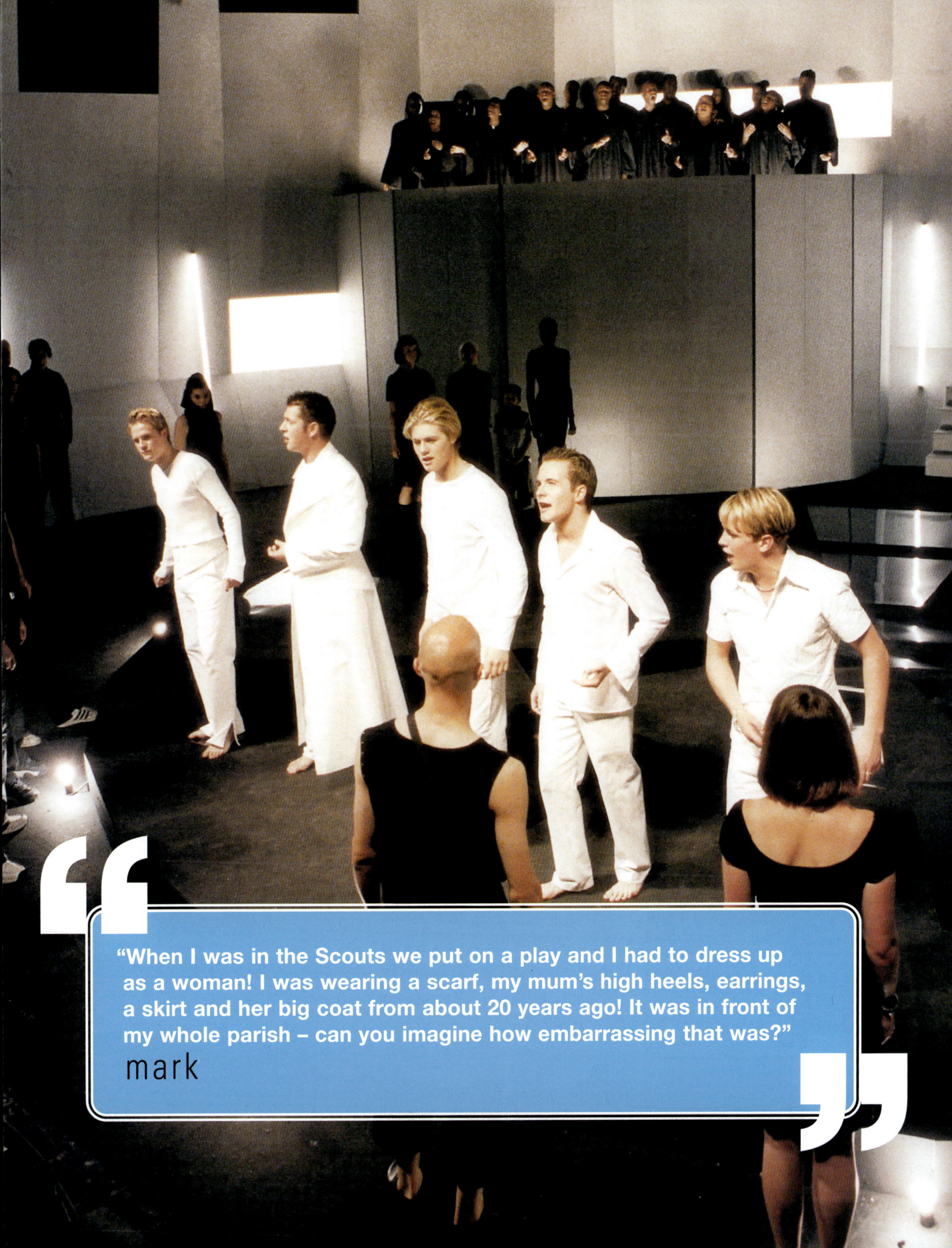

"When I was in the Scouts we put on a play and I had to dress up as a woman! I was wearing a scarf, my mum's high heels, earrings, a skirt and her big coat from about 20 years ago! It was in front of my whole parish – can you imagine how embarrassing that was?"

mark

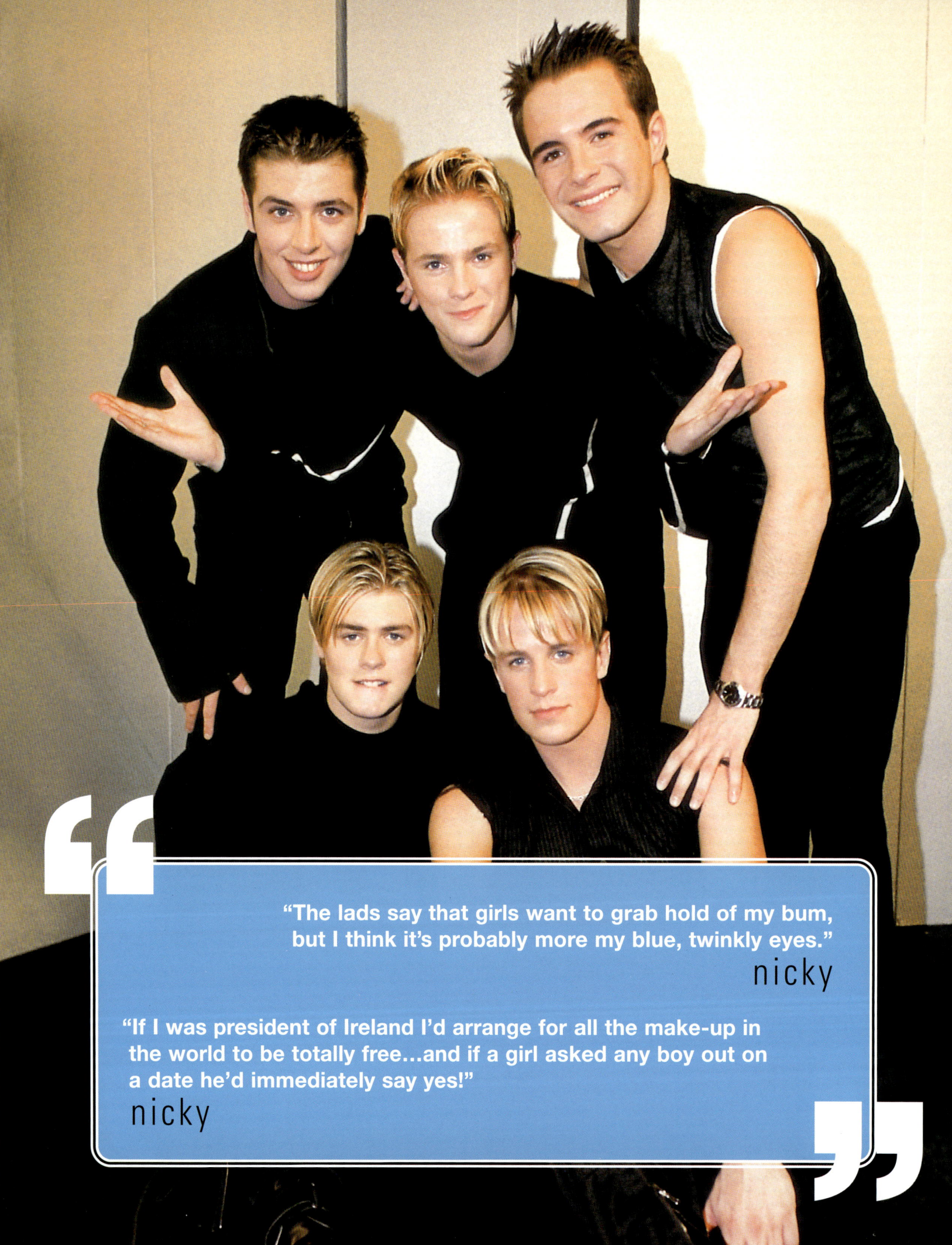

"The lads say that girls want to grab hold of my bum, but I think it's probably more my blue, twinkly eyes."

nicky

"If I was president of Ireland I'd arrange for all the make-up in the world to be totally free...and if a girl asked any boy out on a date he'd immediately say yes!"

nicky

"When I was about 17 and living in Leeds, myself and three other lads from Dublin told these girls we were in a new Irish boy band called OTT, cos it was around the time OTT were just about to hit Britain. And they believed us! They asked us if we knew Boyzone and we pretended we did. They even asked us for our autographs! In a way though it wasn't so much of a lie but a premonition – 'cos three years later, I *am* in an Irish boy band and I *do* know Boyzone!"

nicky

"I'm not into eating extravagant food. I've never tried lobster or caviar. If I tried caviar I think it'd put me off my food and I'd be very upset. Once I tried sushi and I hated it."

shane

"I was in a holiday centre where this event called the Community Games was taking place. It must have been around midnight and I was sitting on this railing out on a balcony which was a bit wet. Next thing you know, my foot slipped and I fell back. Luckily enough my foot got caught in a clothes line which broke my fall. I fell head-first about two storeys and I was still knocked unconscious with a dislocated shoulder. Who knows what would have happened without that washing line?!"

kian

"I bite my fingernails and spit them out. I once spat off a roof and hit someone. I didn't mean to, but it was a direct hit."

bryan

"My auntie has a new-born kitten and it was gorgeous, I was cuddling it and I wouldn't let it go. Next thing I knew it had weed all over my smart top that I was wearing to go out for lunch!"

mark

"I'm young, free and single. So if there's anyone out there! Seriously it is very hard to have girlfriends as we are away so much – that's the reality of it, and it's going to be worse before it gets better."

shane

"A few months ago I was always asking Louis, 'When are we going to do this, when are we going to do that?' and he said, 'Look Kian, in a year's time you'll be asking me when will we have a day off?'"

kian

"I've worked in a cash and carry store, a wine cellar and McDonalds, which was by far the worst. I was a security guard for McDonalds in Dublin City Centre and it was awful. I just stood there all day – it was so boring."

bryan

"We want to be the biggest band in the world – that's our dream.
We don't really see it as taking over from anybody else, though."

mark

"I'm probably the bravest when it comes to trying stuff. I love Japanese, Italian and Thai food. But the other guys are like, 'Nah, just give me burger and chips please!' There's a lot of stuff I don't like though, I tried snails in France and they were horrid! I'm a bit wary of seafood – a lot of it can react with you and kill you in seconds!"

nicky

"

"I felt weird wearing stage make-up for the first time. I was dead paranoid about it. I thought, 'Is everyone staring at me, is it obvious?'"

shane

"I used to have a toy cat called Kitty. It wasn't a pink cat but it wasn't a black cat either, if you know what I mean. It was something a girl would definitely have had. I'd hide him under the bed when my friends came round."

shane

"

westlife
discography

singles

Together Girl Forever
(as IOU)
Together Girl Forever
Everlasting Love
Together Girl Forever
(Instrumental)
Everlasting Love (Instrumental)
Release date:
December 1998 (Eire only)
Highest chart position: Did not chart

Swear It Again
CD1:
Swear It Again (Radio Edit)
Forever
CD-Rom
CD2: (Limited Edition)
Swear It Again (Radio Edit)
Swear It Again (Rockstone Mix)
Interview with Ronan Keating
Release date: April 1999
Highest chart position: Number 1

Swear It Again EP
Swear It Again
Until The End Of Time
Forever
Everybody Knows
Let's Make Tonight Special
Don't Calm The Storm
Interview with Ronan Keating
Release date: April 1999
Highest chart position:
N/A (limited edition)

If I Let You Go
CD1:
If I Let You Go (radio edit)
Try Again
CD-Rom
CD2:
If I Let You Go (radio edit)
If I Let You Go (extended mix)
Interview with Andi Peters
Release date: August 1999
Highest chart position: Number 1

Flying Without Wings
CD1:
Flying Without Wings
Everybody Knows
CD-Rom
CD2:
Flying Without Wings
That's What It's All About
Flying Without Wings
(Acappella version)
Release date: October 1999
Highest chart position: Number 1

I Have A Dream /
Seasons In The Sun
I Have A Dream
Seasons In The Sun
On The Wings Of Love
Release date: December 1999
Highest chart position: Number 1

Fool Again
Formats TBC
Release date: February 2000
Highest chart position: TBC

album

'Westlife'
Swear It Again
If I Let You Go
Flying Without Wings
Fool Again
No No
I Don't Wanna Fight
Change The World
Moments
Seasons In The Sun
I Need You
Miss You
More Than Words
Open Your Heart
Try Again
What I Want Is What I Got
We Are One
Can't Lose What You Never Had
Release date: November 1999
Highest chart position: Number 2